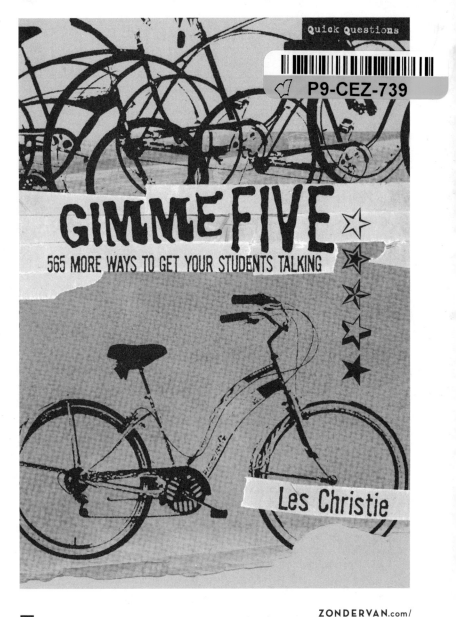

P9-CEZ-739

# GIMME FIVE

## 565 MORE WAYS TO GET YOUR STUDENTS TALKING

### Les Christie

**ZONDERVAN**®

**Youth Specialties**
.com

ZONDERVAN.com/
AUTHORTRACKER
*follow your favorite authors*

**Youth Specialties**

*Gimme Five: 565 Enticing Icebreakers to Get Students Talking, Laughing, and Thinking*
Copyright © 2006 by Les Christie

Youth Specialties products, 300 South Pierce Street, El Cajon, CA 92020 are published by Zondervan, 5300 Patterson Avenue Southeast, Grand Rapids, MI 49530.

---

**Library of Congress Cataloging-in-Publication Data**

Christie, Les John.
  Gimme five : 565 enticing icebreakers to get students talking, laughing, and thinking / Les Christie.
     p. cm.
  ISBN-10: 0-310-27315-3
  ISBN-13: 978-0-310-27315-8
  1. Church work with teenagers. I. Title.
  BV4447.C47742 2006
  268'.433--dc22

                                                          2006015057

---

Web site addresses listed in this book were current at the time of publication. Please contact Youth Specialties via e-mail (YS@YouthSpecialties.com) to report URLs that are no longer operational and replacement URLs if available.

*Creative Team: Dave Urbanski, Kristi Robison, Brad Taylor, Anna Hammond, Ryan Sharp/SharpSeven Design*
*Cover design by Holly Sharp*

Printed in the United States

---

09 10 11 12 • 20 19 18 17 16 15 14 13 12 11 10 9 8 7 6 5 4 3

# DEDICATION

To my two grown sons, Brent and David, who continue to bring joy to my life and my wife Gretchen's life. They allow me to try out on them many of the initial ideas that pop up in many of my books, and for that I am grateful. They are a lot of fun, too, and Gretchen and I so much enjoy their visits and our phone conversations with them.

# ACKNOWLEDGMENTS

This book would not have been possible if it were not for a group of talented and creative people. As with many things in life, this book was a joint venture.

I am so grateful to the many fine folks at YS, including Jay Howver for giving the initial approval to do this book, and for his ongoing support and encouragement. Also, sincere thanks must go to Dave Urbanski and Kristi Robison with their objective comments as they edited the book. I am also very appreciative of Holly Sharp, book cover artist, for allowing me to participate in the cover selection.

I am very thankful to Emily Darlington, faculty projects coordinator at William Jessup University, for again helping with the initial typing of the manuscript. Emily also helped with the indexing. I am also appreciative for the work of Cole Orick, teacher assistant, in helping with the indexing.

Many of the better ideas in this book were contributed by William Jessup University (WJU) students, including Janell Brothers, Katy Cantrell, Aletheia Celio, Jessica Goldsborough, Jon Havens, Ryan Kent, Billy Kessler, Michael La Farge, Robin Matthews, and Michael Matthews (Robin's delightful young son). Andy Palmer, Jessica Spangler, and Allison Bowman (all WJU students) assisted with indexing. Tina Peterson, WJU registrar, contributed helpful opinions and was part of the initial sorting out the best from the good of the many Gimme Fives. I am thankful to my students Katy Cantrell and Jennifer Allivato for their expertise in assisting with the topical index. I also appreciate the clever contributions of three of my Western Seminary students: Jeff Bachman, John Herman, and Jonathan McKee.

# HOW TO GET THE MOST OUT OF *GIMME FIVE*

This collection of icebreakers and discussion starters will cause your teenagers (and even you) to take a deeper look at who they are and what they believe. They will lighten the mood, stimulate discussions, build community, and get kids wrestling with a variety of issues. Among the more than 550 prompts inside are just plain fun icebreakers—some even a little silly. Others are serious and deal with issues many students and adults face. Either way, they're all perfect for the classroom, home, youth group meetings, small group settings, Sunday school, camps and retreats, long trips in a car or bus, classrooms—and more! You can use the material in *Gimme Five* anytime, anywhere.

Have fun with these prompts. Change them, play around with them, add details to them. Use them as points of departure and let your imagination run. Try to express what you're thinking and feeling. These icebreakers should be springboards into memories, thoughts, and experiences. Read them in order or jump around to your heart's content. Use the **word index** and the **topical index** in the back to find the perfect prompt. Ask students to yell out a number and go to that number in the book. Use them for rapid-fire "Q&A" or linger on one and watch the discussion unfold. Some prompts will cause laughter; some may invoke tears. These phrases will get your students laughing, debating, and thinking—and they'll learn a ton about each other in the process.

Some icebreakers are designed to stretch you, some to push you out of your comfort zone. Some force you to make difficult choices. Don't be afraid of them. Think. Use your creativity. Dream.

You may want to code your favorite prompts as well. For example, write an **F** next to icebreakers you think are funny and know will get

a laugh; write a **DD** next to prompts you know will cause the group to dig deeper in the conversation; write an **HT** next to hot topics that will inspire debate.

This book can also complement a study on a particular topic. There are two helpful indexes in back in case you're looking for specific words or topics.

Be wise in deciding which icebreakers to use. Hopefully you know your group members well enough to know which prompts from *Gimme Five* are and aren't appropriate. So be sensitive to the issues your group members may be facing.

In a small group setting you may want to begin by having your students sit in a circle so you can toss out some of the lighter icebreakers. Then, going clockwise around the circle, have each student offer one response to the *Gimme Five* prompt you selected until each person has had a chance to respond. Then allow anyone in the group to offer additional answers. Have your students talk about the processes they went through to come up with their responses, including whether the prompts helped them remember any life experiences.

It's amazing how often kids respond to icebreakers in ways we never would have predicted. Part of the enjoyment of the icebreakers is discovering the journeys they take to come up with their responses.

As you approach each icebreaker, consider possible follow-up questions (I provide a few examples throughout the book). Explore

all the possibilities. Brainstorm ways to approach the questions. Ask yourself why you selected them. *If you were in a different time or place, would you still have responded in the same way? Why or why not? What if you were with different people? How might they affect your reactions?*

You can use the prompts in this book for games (similar to the classic game "Categories")—the competitive process will add excitement. First choose a prompt, this time using the phrase "Gimme five or more…" Then give students about two minutes to write down as many answers as they can. Then ask students one at a time to reveal their responses to the group. Each answer a student comes up with that one or more group members also come up with earns one point. Each answer that no one else writes down earns two points. And so on. You can also make up your own rules if you want. But do have students share why they thought of those answers, including any life experiences that relate to their answers.

You can also take this book on a solo journey. Get away for an hour or a day or a weekend by yourself. Find a comfortable place where you won't be disturbed and then dive into the prompts. One of the benefits of this book is that it allows you to gain insights without actually living through the predicaments described. You may want to record some of your thoughts to look at later or to share with a friend.

I hope *Gimme Five* raises questions you have wanted to tackle for a long time, and I hope you have an exceptional experience!

—L.C.

# GIMME FIVE

**1**

Gimme five inappropriate times to laugh hysterically

**2**

Gimme five flu symptoms

**3**

Gimme five of your favorite family traditions

**4**

Gimme five of the worst pets

**5**

Gimme five of the worst places to have hair on your body

**6**

Gimme five smells in your grandparents' house

**7**

Gimme five bands with at least one male and two female members

**8**

Gimme five TV shows that never should've been cancelled

**9**

Gimme five ways to serve an egg

**10**

Gimme five desserts you love

## 11

Gimme five types of "bad news" stories on TV

### FOLLOW-UPS:

What percentage of the news is "bad news"?

How do you feel about the amount of bad news on TV?

Would you watch more TV news if there were more good news?

More bad news?

Why do networks report so much bad news?

## 12

Gimme five names you should never give a dog

## 13

Gimme five dream jobs

**14**

Gimme five of the lamest superhero names

**15**

Gimme five activities with age requirements

**16**

Gimme five summer jobs you wish you never took

**17**

Gimme five objects you shouldn't take into the bathtub

**18**

Gimme five possessions people often forget to pack

**19**

Gimme five objects that wash up on the beach

**20**

Gimme five vegetables people plant in their gardens

**21**

What is an appropriate curfew for a teenager?

## FOLLOW-UPS:

Why is this time more appropriate than other times?

What about for a 13-year-old versus a 17-year-old?

What do you think about the concept of curfews?

**22**

Gimme five famous TV fathers

**23**

Gimme five occasions that require reservations

**24**

Gimme five types of trees in a typical neighborhood

**25**

Gimme five free items you would find in a hotel room

**26**

Gimme five of the most significant choices people make in their lives

# GIMME FIVE

## 27

Gimme five brands of toothpaste

## 28

Gimme five items that can be purchased in a tube

## 29

Gimme five objects dogs bark at

## 30

Gimme five places where you might hear people applauding

## 31

Gimme five kinds of vehicles you or your family have owned over the years

**FOLLOW-UPS:**

How many years do people typically keep a new vehicle?

What's your favorite car and why?

What will transportation look like in the future?

## 32

Gimme five liquids that come in a spray bottle

## 33

Gimme five situations that call for hand washing

## 34

Gimme five objects that bear your school insignia or mascot

**35**

Gimme five situations in which people get furious with complete strangers

**36**

Gimme five animals you would recognize just by their sounds

**37**

Gimme five English words you can form using some or all of the letters in the word *planets*

**38**

Gimme five games to play in a supermarket

**39**

Gimme five foods you should not eat if you have an upset stomach

**40**

Gimme five items people use after sneezing if they can't find tissue

**41**

Gimme five ages you're looking forward to

**FOLLOW-UPS:**

At what age do people go from middle age to old age?

Why did you select that age?

How can you tell if a person is "old"?

How will you respond to this question when you're 20
years older?

**42**

Gimme five magazines with one-word titles

**43**

Gimme five objects people feel the need to touch before they buy

**44**

Gimme five subjects people consider "personal"

**45**

Gimme five power tools

**46**

Gimme five people in a courtroom

**47**

Gimme five foods people keep in their refrigerators too long

**48**

Gimme five pro sports teams with birds as their mascots

**49**

Gimme five of the best-tasting pies

**50**

Gimme five reality TV shows

**51**

Gimme five ages when it's ideal to marry

## FOLLOW-UPS:

How do you know you've fallen in love?

In some countries parents select their child's spouse; do you
think your parents would make a wise choice?

How many times do people fall in love before they marry?

**52**

Gimme five things a five-year-old might pray for

**53**

Gimme five items connected with a lifeguard

**54**

Gimme five objects people place on Christmas trees

**55**

Gimme five varieties of soup

**56**

Gimme five American companies recognized all over the world

**57**

Gimme five movie sequels

**58**

Gimme five types of sauces

**59**

Gimme five clubs a high schooler might join

**60**

Gimme five nursery-rhyme characters

**61**

Gimme five "rites of passage" for a guy (or girl) transitioning into adulthood

# GIMME FIVE

**62**

Gimme five things people do when they're stuck in traffic

**63**

Gimme five objects you rent (or people you hire) for a wedding

**64**

Gimme five appliances found in most homes

**65**

Gimme five TV shows broadcast once a year

**66**

Gimme five things people do while sleeping

**67**

Gimme five TV mothers

**68**

Gimme five foods people put peanut butter on

**69**

Gimme five animals or insects living in your backyard

**70**

Gimme five Summer Olympic events

## 71

Gimme five situations in which emotions are hardest to hide

**FOLLOW-UPS:**

What are the hardest emotions for you to experience?

What if humans didn't show emotions—what kind of world would

we live in?

Do you think your pets have emotions? If yes, list them.

How do you think God views our emotions?

## 72

Gimme five items people put on bulletin boards

## 73

Gimme five minimum—wage jobs

**74**

Gimme five words or phrases salespeople use to seal the deal

**75**

Gimme five of the worst jobs

**76**

Gimme five drinks that taste best cold

**77**

Gimme five types of meat found in a supermarket

**78**

Gimme five explanations people give for not wanting to go to work

# GIMME FIVE

**79**

Gimme five reasons for moving to America

**80**

Gimme five kids' games adults still like to play

**81**

Gimme five great novels

**82**

Gimme five body parts people modify with plastic surgery

**83**

Gimme five activities people put on their to-do lists before going on vacation

## 84

Gimme five items that siblings might have to share

## 85

Gimme five animated Disney movies

## 86

Gimme five TV series in reruns

## 87

Gimme five attributes for a single guy (or girl) that would impress the opposite sex

## 88

Gimme five instruments in a full orchestra

**89**

Gimme five objects considered acceptable to stare at

**90**

Gimme five sports that require protective gear

**91**

Gimme five times during the day when a female might apply makeup

## FOLLOW-UPS:

What types of makeup are your favorites?

How old should a girl be before she's allowed to use makeup?

**92**

Gimme five businesses that ask shoppers to "take a number"

## 93

Gimme five terms or phrases beginning with the word *power*

## 94

Gimme five words or phrases people say to their pets

## 95

Gimme five types of hats

## 96

Gimme five brands of soda

## 97

Gimme five places where strangers have to sit next to each other

**98**

Gimme five synonyms for the overused word *great*

**99**

Gimme five uncomfortable situations for you

**100**

Gimme five expressions kids use to describe something disgusting

**101**

Gimme five Bible stories you wish you could have witnessed

**102**

Gimme five New Year's resolutions

## 103

Gimme five activities teenagers participate in that irritate their parents

## 104

Gimme five of the most expensive purchases a person ever makes

## 105

Gimme five greetings that don't require words

## 106

Gimme five animals that would make boring pets

## 107

Gimme five items for which men/women enjoy shopping

**108**

Gimme five objects you fill with water

**109**

Gimme five exercises people do at home

**110**

Gimme five types of improper behavior that cause parents to send children to their rooms

**111**

Gimme five ways to relieve a headache

**112**

Gimme five items or activities connected with July 4

**113**

Gimme five objects people keep in junk drawers

**114**

Gimme five types of cheese

**115**

Gimme five events with really expensive tickets

**116**

Gimme five of the grossest ice cream flavors

**117**

Gimme five activities/projects people start but don't always finish

**118**

Gimme five creatures that lay eggs

**119**

Gimme five salad-bar ingredients you never use

**120**

Gimme five things in people's minds when they daydream

**121**

Gimme five brands of shampoo

**122**

Gimme five objects in a car's glove compartment

**123**

Gimme five fads that have come and gone

**124**

Gimme five shows on Nick at Nite

**125**

Gimme five things you put on your hair

**126**

Gimme five really loud places

**127**

Gimme five cars that cost more than 50 grand

**128**

Gimme five college football bowl games

## 129

Gimme five foods on which people put whipped cream

## 130

Gimme five fears or phobias

## 131

Gimme five illegal things that some would like legalized

**FOLLOW-UPS:**

How would you rate this list in order of importance for those who want them legalized?

How do you feel about these issues?

How do you express your feelings about these issues?

**132**

Gimme five jobs that start with the letter "T"

**133**

Gimme five items people put in the backyard

**134**

Gimme five phrases or expressions that include the word good

**135**

Gimme five objects regularly ripped off

**136**

Gimme five historical figures you'd love to meet

**137**

Gimme five things you'd find on a map

**138**

Gimme five household items people typically run out of

**139**

Gimme five things money cannot buy

**140**

Gimme five ice-cream flavors you hope no one ever invents

**141**

Gimme five reasons a person quits a job

# GIMME FIVE

**FOLLOW-UPS:**

How many years do most people hold a job?

How many jobs does the average person have over a lifetime?

What are the qualities/characteristics of a good employee?

Why do some people stay a long time at one job and

others don't?

## 142

Gimme five cities or provinces in Canada

## 143

Gimme five locations where people must be very quiet

## 144

Gimme five items in a safe-deposit box

**145**

Gimme five problems people have with their dogs

**146**

Gimme five individuals who wear masks as part of their jobs

**147**

Gimme five yummy foods for a midnight snack

**148**

Gimme five items people put away at the end of summer

**149**

Gimme five items you pour or shake on food

## 150

Gimme five sounds you hear in a haunted house

## 151

Gimme five brand names of energy drinks

## 152

Gimme five causes of itchy skin

## 153

Gimme five games to pass the time in a car

## 154

Gimme five of the best excuses for cutting a class

## 155

Gimme five synonyms for the word *strange*

## 156

Gimme five comments wives (or husbands) like to hear from their spouses

## 157

Gimme five Christmas carols you'd find in a hymnal (i.e., not "Jingle Bells")

## 158

Gimme five objects you'd find on the floor of a young boy's (or girl's) room

## 159

Gimme five appropriate occasions to give flowers

## 160

Gimme five types of gear you take camping

## 161

Gimme five names of rich/wealthy people

### FOLLOW-UPS:

How much money do you need to be considered rich in America?

What is the most money a family could make and still be

considered poor in America?

How does this compare with families in other countries?

## 162

Gimme five difficulties people have with their hair

# GIMME FIVE

**163**

Gimme five signs that a storm is approaching

**164**

Gimme five names of rap artists

**165**

Gimme five places children don't enjoy going

**166**

Gimme five ways to serve a potato

**167**

Gimme five personal belongings people typically misplace

**168**

Gimme five James Bond movies

45

**169**

Gimme five of the worst-tasting foods you've eaten

**170**

Gimme five sports that take the most toll on the body

## FOLLOW-UPS:

What age is considered old for an athlete?

In what sports do people improve with age?

What sports can you participate in for most of your life?

**171**

Gimme five activities you do on a boring day

**172**

Gimme five of the dustiest objects found in attics

**173**

Gimme five ways to boost the value of a home

**174**

Gimme five swimming pool games

**175**

Gimme five places students go on class trips

**176**

Gimme five objects that would hardly make a sound if you dropped them

## 177

Gimme five of the most common exclamations used in everyday conversation

## 178

Gimme five foods a health fanatic would never eat

## 179

Gimme five synonyms for the word *intelligent*

## 180

Gimme five cars you would buy if money were no object

## FOLLOW-UPS:

Of the five cars you chose, which would you drive often and which would you keep in storage under heavy security?

How much money does the average person spend on a car?

What do you think about going into debt to purchase a car?

How long should people take to pay off their car loans?

## 181

Gimme five belongings thieves steal from cars

## 182

Gimme five of your favorite spaces on a Monopoly board

## 183

Gimme five activities you're scared to attempt even though they seem fun

**184**

Gimme five types of cats

**185**

Gimme five objects in a bathroom

**186**

Gimme five of the funniest-looking animals in a zoo

**187**

Gimme five objects that rattle

**188**

Gimme five things that bring tears to your eyes

**189**

Gimme five things that have endings

**190**

Gimme five excuses you've used after oversleeping

## FOLLOW-UPS:

How long does it take you to get out of the house quickly when you wake up late?

What's the average time people go to bed?

If you go to bed earlier, do you wake up earlier?

How does your bedtime change as you grow older?

How much sleep do you need to function well the next day?

**191**

Gimme five scenarios that frighten you

## 192

Gimme five items you wouldn't miss if you were stranded on an island

## 193

Gimme five buildings you can name by just looking at them

## 194

Gimme five of the most popular dance moves

## 195

Gimme five objects that go round and round

## 196

Gimme five synonyms for the word *pal*

## 197

Gimme five sounds you might hear on a farm

## 198

Gimme five animals you've eaten

## 199

Gimme five presents people who are in love give each other

## 200

Gimme five legal activities that some people want to outlaw

## FOLLOW-UPS:

Why do some people want these outlawed?

How would you rate this list in order of importance for those who want them outlawed?

Have you ever told people your thoughts on these issues?

## 201
Gimme five things that live below the ground

## 202
Gimme five synonyms for the word *large*

## 203
Gimme five items you find in the Yellow Pages

## 204
Gimme five words or phrases used in court

# GIMME FIVE

## 205

Gimme five foods that taste awful when not combined with other foods

## 206

Gimme five items people accidentally leave on airplanes

## 207

Gimme five foods with very few calories

## 208

Gimme five objects made to be stepped or walked on

## 209

Gimme five saltwater fish

## 210

Gimme the names of five women (or men) you consider tall

**FOLLOW-UPS:**

What is the ideal height for a woman (or man)?

What year did you grow the most, and how did that make

you feel?

How does your height compare to your parents' statures?

## 211

Gimme five activities people do when they first arrive at work

## 212

Gimme five attributes/qualities that make a person popular

# GIMME FIVE

**213**

Gimme five sticky items

**214**

Gimme five words or phrases people use to get others to come to the dinner table

**215**

Gimme five objects with electrical cords

**216**

Gimme five ways parents reward their kids

**217**

Gimme five commands you give a dog

**218**

Gimme five types of pies without fruit

**219**

Gimme five games you play standing or sitting in a circle

**220**

Gimme five of the most boring sports to watch on TV

## FOLLOW-UPS:

What makes these sports so boring to watch on TV?

What can be done to make them more exciting for TV?

Have you ever played any of these sports? If so, are they more exciting to play?

**221**

Gimme five things you buy at the concession stand before watching a movie

**222**

Gimme five decisions people make every day

**223**

Gimme five items used mostly in summer

**224**

Gimme five cartoon characters that wear capes

**225**

Gimme five foods associated with Christmas

**226**

Gimme five enjoyable places to spend a rainy afternoon

**227**

Gimme five ways to say "Get out of here!"

**228**

Gimme five occasions when people send greeting cards

**229**

Gimme five items people donate to charity

**230**

Gimme five examples of things you've always dreamed of owning

# GIMME FIVE

## 231

Gimme five things people compliment other people on

## 232

Gimme five Starbucks drinks

## 233

Gimme five exciting moments during your typical school day

**234**

Gimme five ways people show appreciation

**235**

Gimme five Ben & Jerry's ice cream flavors

**236**

Gimme five occasions when people have their pictures taken

**237**

Gimme five jobs that get you dirty

**238**

Gimme five bedtime stories children love to hear

**239**

Gimme five sports you would like to see in the Olympics

**240**

Gimme five things you do to get ready for your day

**FOLLOW-UPS:**

How much time do you allow for each thing you have to do?

Which is the most important task?

**241**

Gimme five accounts people open

**242**

Gimme five objects a cat enjoys

## 243

Gimme five names you would give a cat

## 244

Gimme five sports that should be outlawed from the Olympics

## 245

Gimme five places to hide when playing hide-and-seek

## 246

Gimme five reasons students give for dropping out of college/high school

## 247

Gimme five places you might have difficulty finding a seat

**248**

Gimme five crunchy snack foods

**249**

Gimme five things you wish you could invent

**250**

Gimme five of your favorite brands/kinds of footwear

## FOLLOW-UPS:

How long does a pair of shoes last for you?

What do you do that causes shoes to wear out?

How many pair of shoes do you own?

What is so special about your favorite pair?

## 251

Gimme five things a school nurse does for a sick student

## 252

Gimme five places you go when you have a lot on your mind

## 253

Gimme five reasons you might stay up past your typical bedtime

## 254

Gimme five situations that call for a flashlight

## 255

Gimme five characteristics of an undesirable roommate

**256**

Gimme five activities your parents might criticize you for doing too quickly (or slowly)

**257**

Gimme five items in a high schooler's backpack

**258**

Gimme five jobs that may require working on Christmas day

**259**

Gimme five occasions when a grown-up might seek parental advice

**260**

Gimme five circumstances that require you stay up all night

## FOLLOW-UPS:

What's the minimum amount of sleep you need?

Describe how well you function on that amount of sleep.

Are you a morning, afternoon, or evening person?

How often do you sleep in?

How long after your alarm goes off do you actually get out
of bed?

### 261

Gimme five movies starring _____
(name any actor or actress)

### 262

Gimme five objects children like to climb on

### 263

Gimme five healthy foods

## 264

Gimme five of your favorite MySpace pages

**FOLLOW-UPS:**

What kind of stuff is being posted on MySpace?

What are your friends looking for on MySpace?

What are the benefits of MySpace?

What are the dangers of MySpace?

## 265

Gimme five items in a hospital

## 266

Gimme five places parents take children on Sundays

## 267

Gimme five items that should be fresh when you buy them

## 268

Gimme five sports in which people toss something

## 269

Gimme five objects in a birdcage

## 270

Gimme five things that come in threes

## 271

Gimme five places parents say babies come from

**272**

Gimme five typical wedding gifts

**273**

Gimme five places pets are prohibited

**274**

Gimme five things you can do to make a sore throat feel better

**275**

Gimme five foods you'd love to eat every day

**276**

Gimme five words nothing rhymes with

**277**

Gimme five things teenagers do when angry at their parents

**278**

Gimme five items people store in their basements

**279**

Gimme five reasons some people have a difficult time sleeping

**280**

Gimme five reasons the speed limit makes sense

**FOLLOW~UPS:**

Should there be a national speed limit? At what speed would you

set it?

Why would you set it at this speed?

Do you think some people would still drive faster than the

speed limit?

## 281

Gimme five cookies you enjoy eating

## 282

Gimme five people who wear crowns/tiaras

## 283

Gimme five foods you can identify by their smell when cooking

**284**

Gimme five biblical names people give to newborns

**285**

Gimme five magazines that often use celebrity faces on their covers

**286**

Gimme five things you dislike doing with your family

**287**

Gimme five things you can do with a pumpkin

**288**

Gimme five items in kids' lunchboxes

## 289

Gimme five objects you open

## 290

Gimme five reasons people wait longer to get married today

**FOLLOW-UPS:**

What is the ideal age to get married?

Why did you select that age?

Should the man be older or younger than the woman?

How old were your parents when they got married?

Do you think the age you get married determines if you
get divorced?

Is there always a relationship between age and maturity?

## 291

Gimme five things you put on the surface of a cake

## 292

Gimme five things you like doing with your family

## 293

Gimme five instruments you won't find in a marching band

## 294

Gimme five of the worst Christmas gifts

## 295

Gimme five small animals that frighten people

**296**

Gimme five foods that taste good with melted cheese

**297**

Gimme five activities children often forget to do

**298**

Gimme five household chores you dread

**299**

Gimme five objects in a classroom

**300**

Gimme five names of supermodels

**301**

Gimme five things you see at the circus

**302**

Gimme five car parts

**303**

Gimme five fairy-tale characters who fall in love

**304**

Gimme five things that make your heart beat faster

**305**

Gimme five items for which you shop before buying

**306**

Gimme five gentle breeds of dogs

**307**

Gimme five jobs that require special shoes

**308**

Gimme five places where people dress up

**309**

Gimme five games people play at picnics

**310**

Gimme five reasons not to date

## FOLLOW-UPS:

At what age do people start dating?

Are most people ready to date at this age?

How old should they be?

What are the benefits of dating?

## 311

Gimme five ice-cream toppings

## 312

Gimme five items people throw away every day

## 313

Gimme five things parents tell teenagers not to waste

# GIMME FIVE

**314**

Gimme five parts of a book

**315**

Gimme five Looney Tunes characters

**316**

Gimme five holidays

**317**

Gimme five animated Disney characters

**318**

Gimme five things you do when you're sick

**319**

Gimme five synonyms for the word *house*

## 320

Gimme five scary movies involving baby-sitters

**FOLLOW-UPS:**

When is a person old enough to baby-sit?

Have you ever been a baby-sitter? If so, what was that like?

What is the average pay for baby-sitting? Is that enough?

What is the most difficult part of baby-sitting?

At what age is a child ready to be left alone, without a
    baby-sitter?

What makes a child ready to be left alone at this age?

Are there other things to consider besides age?

When did your parents start letting you stay home alone?

## 321

Gimme five Dr. Seuss characters

**322**

Gimme five excuses you use to get off the phone

**323**

Gimme five current Saturday-morning cartoons

**324**

Gimme five cars you'd like to drive for a day

**325**

Gimme five pizza toppings

**326**

Gimme five airport jobs

### 327

Gimme five of the most famous athletes from outside the United States

### 328

Gimme five ways to lift a bad mood

### 329

Gimme five things teenagers' parents worry about

### 330

Gimme five countries on the equator

### 331

Gimme five gym exercises

## 332

Gimme five things people do or say to let someone of the opposite sex know they are "interested"

## 333

Gimme five areas married couples disagree on while divorcing

**FOLLOW-UPS:**

Do you think most divorcing couples tried hard enough to

stay together?

If you have friends with divorced parents, share how they cope...

Is there ever a bright side to divorce?

## 334

Gimme five activities you should only do very cautiously

**335**

Gimme five items a clown might put on

**336**

Gimme five things parents say that make teenagers groan

**337**

Gimme five items people have on their key chains

**338**

Gimme five things we do naturally (without thinking about them)

**339**

Gimme five things you might find under a rock

## 340

Gimme five celebrities who look great with gray hair

**FOLLOW-UPS:**

At what age do people start growing gray hair?

Why do some people color their gray hair?

What do you think when you see a person with gray hair?

## 341

Gimme five words you would use to describe God

## 342

Gimme five things you would like to have more of

343

Gimme five things passed down as family keepsakes

344

Gimme five nervous/annoying habits people have

345

Gimme five items people buy on a whim

346

Gimme five places people leave when they get bored

347

Gimme five places that usually have long lines

88

**348**

Gimme five reasons people wake up really early in the morning

**349**

Gimme five activities people with a fear of heights are not likely to do

**350**

Gimme five reasons not to own a cell phone

**FOLLOW-UPS:**

How many minutes a month do you spend on the phone?

Do you prefer text messaging over speaking?

Do you remember rotary phones? If so, have you ever used one?

## 351

Gimme five items teenagers pressure their parents to buy for them

## 352

Gimme five things that make you sneeze

## 353

Gimme five things a baby would say if he or she could talk

## 354

Gimme five items associated with Cinderella

## 355

Gimme five major clothing companies

# GIMME FIVE

**356**

Gimme five things that can make a teacher unpopular

**357**

Gimme five reasons you might want to stay after school

**358**

Gimme five objects people place on nightstands when they go to bed

**359**

Gimme five animals that you'd like to be for an hour (but not a week)

**360**

Gimme the names of five men (or women) you consider short

## FOLLOW-UPS:

What's the average height for a man (or woman)?

What's the ideal height for a man (or woman)?

Is it better to be of average height or uniquely short?

**361**

Gimme five jobs little boys/girls pretend to have

**362**

Gimme five kinds of doughnuts

**363**

Gimme five items you would take from your house if it were on fire

**364**

Gimme five foods people put ketchup on

**365**

Gimme five things that make a restaurant one of your favorites

**366**

Gimme five words or phrases you might hear in a prayer

**367**

Gimme five irritating things people do on airplanes

**368**

Gimme five things you hate to see come to an end

## 369

Gimme five things you would do if you were locked out of your car

## 370

Gimme five birthday presents you would love to receive

### FOLLOW-UPS:

What was your favorite birthday present so far?

What was your favorite birthday party so far?

## 371

Gimme five TV shows featuring an animal

## 372

Gimme five foods you eat with crackers

# GIMME FIVE

**373**

Gimme five activities people procrastinate before doing

**374**

Gimme five things people do when saying good-bye

**375**

Gimme five words that rhyme with *link*

**376**

Gimme five comic book characters

**377**

Gimme five objects you see in the sky

**378**

Gimme five things you do for a baby

**379**

Gimme five places people hide keys

**380**

Gimme five of the longest car/van trips you've taken

### FOLLOW-UPS:

How many hours of driving makes a car trip long?

What was your worst long car trip?

What was your favorite long car trip?

Where do you like to sit on long car trips?

**381**

Gimme five objects you'd find in a church

**382**

Gimme five members of the Baseball Hall of Fame

**383**

Gimme five things on a farm

**384**

Gimme five movies that were supposed to be funny but weren't

**385**

Gimme five items people put on bookshelves besides books

**386**

Gimme five objects in a purse

**387**

Gimme five promises a political candidate might make

**388**

Gimme five animals mentioned in the Bible

**389**

Gimme five things you light with a match

**390**

Gimme five ways to prevent your body from "going downhill" when you get older

# GIMME FIVE

## FOLLOW-UPS:

At what age does your body start going downhill?

What is a sign your body is going downhill?

Do you know an older person whose body is not going downhill?

## 391

Gimme five expensive objects a very wealthy person might have

## 392

Gimme five items people borrow

## 393

Gimme five things associated with Halloween

## 394

Gimme five items people place on rearview mirrors

**395**

Gimme five foods you buy more than just one of

**396**

Gimme five modes of transportation

**397**

Gimme five places you aren't supposed to skate

**398**

Gimme five things teenagers envy about each other

**399**

Gimme five items you might bring to a sick friend

## 400

Gimme five of the largest families (counting parents and children) you've met

**FOLLOW-UPS:**

How many kids should a married couple have?

How long should a married couple wait before having a baby?

Why did you select this amount of time?

People are having children later in life—how do you feel

about this?

## 401

Gimme five objects you would not want next to your home

## 402

Gimme five things you treat yourself to when you're feeling down

**403**

Gimme five ways to send a message

**404**

Gimme five foods you've never tasted

**405**

Gimme five places where you see more kids than adults

**406**

Gimme five people who might ask for your ID

**407**

Gimme five things served with pancakes

**408**

Gimme five things you do or say to cheer someone up

**409**

Gimme five items associated with England

**410**

Gimme five reasons it's important to take care of your teeth

## FOLLOW-UPS:

Did the "tooth fairy" leave you money when you were younger?

If so, how much?

What did you spend it on?

## 411

Gimme five great places to go on a first date

## 412

Gimme five vegetables you can't eat in one bite

## 413

Gimme five foods that taste better the second day

## 414

Gimme five things people put in a sandwich

## 415

Gimme five jobs not suited for a clumsy person

**416**

Gimme five ways to stop a fish from smelling (see if your kids get the joke, too)

**417**

Gimme five things that can spoil a vacation

**418**

Gimme five movies you've seen more than once

**419**

Gimme five things you give thanks for in your prayers

**420**

Gimme five topics teenagers talk about on the phone

## FOLLOW-UPS:

What's the average amount of time a teenager talks on the phone each day?

How long is your typical phone call?

Who do you usually talk to on the phone?

What means of communication do people use most—phone, e-mail, or talk in person?

## 421

Gimme five ways you can tell a date is going really badly

## 422

Gimme five things that can mess up an evening at the movies

### 423

Gimme five things a customer might do to get back at a bad-mannered waitperson

### 424

Gimme five countries with names that rhyme (fully or partially) with *plan*

### 425

Gimme five things in our culture that corrupt youth

### 426

Gimme five animals easy to imitate in charades

### 427

Gimme five things people put on a hamburger

**428**

Gimme five ways to annoy your brother or sister for an entire family road trip

**429**

Gimme five occasions when you would give a present

**430**

Gimme five of the most common reasons you would leave a note for someone

## FOLLOW-UPS:

Where's the best place to leave a note at home?

Why did you pick this location?

Are you a detailed note writer or a brief note writer?

When people have left you notes, and you missed them, where

were the notes left?

**431**

Gimme five games kids play at recess

**432**

Gimme five ways to say "I love you" without speaking

**433**

Gimme five foods you would cook when feeding a lot of people

**434**

Gimme five euphemisms for "going to the bathroom"

**435**

Gimme five fun and free activities

**436**

Gimme five activities you dislike doing alone

**437**

Gimme five birthday presents you loved as a kid

**438**

Gimme five pieces of clothing people wear that begin with "S"

**439**

Gimme five items young people take with them when they move out of the house

**440**

Gimme five favorite pets you've owned

**FOLLOW-UPS:**

How much reward money would you offer for the return of your

lost pet?

What makes your pet(s) so special?

## 441

Gimme five places kids hide when they're in trouble with their parents

## 442

Gimme five reasons a boss gets mad at an employee

## 443

Gimme five things people who drive with one hand might be doing with their other hand

**444**

Gimme five cordless things you can buy

**445**

Gimme five objects made to attach to a bicycle

**446**

Gimme five things people do when they lose their dogs

**447**

Gimme five things you keep near your bed when you're sick

**448**

Gimme five things never to say to a police officer

**449**

Gimme five things people do to save energy

**450**

Gimme five reasons it's good for guys and girls to be friends

## FOLLOW-UPS:

Are you closer to your guy friends or girl friends?

Have you ever dated a friend?

Can you still be friends after a breakup?

**451**

Gimme five things to do while waiting in line at the supermarket

**452**

Gimme five bands that should've never formed

**453**

Gimme five films that scared the snot out of you

**454**

Gimme five helpful things to have if you're lost at sea

**455**

Gimme five things you shouldn't do if your hands are dirty

**456**

Gimme five celebrities you'd love to eat lunch with

**457**

Gimme five words that describe your parents

**458**

Gimme five symptoms that mean you're getting sick

**459**

Gimme five things people do to stay awake

**460**

Gimme five reasons it's good to move out of the house after you turn 18

## FOLLOW-UPS:

At what age do people become self-supporting?

How and why has this changed in the last 100 years?

Do you think this age differs depending on the country you're in?

How much money do you think a person needs to make every year

to be self-supporting?

## 461

Gimme five appliances you would recognize by their sounds

## 462

Gimme five differences between guys' and girls' bedrooms

## 463

Gimme five unusual pets

**464**

Gimme five activities hard to do without a mirror

**465**

Gimme five personality quirks you don't want your friends to have

**466**

Gimme five key ingredients that enhance a good relationship

**467**

Gimme five extras people want on their cars

**468**

Gimme five road signs many people ignore

## 469

Gimme five things that almost always make you feel sad

## 470

Gimme five things that make you angry

**FOLLOW-UPS:**

How long does it take you to cool down after being angry?

Besides time, what else helps you get over anger?

How do you behave when you're angry?

## 471

Gimme five items people put on their refrigerator doors

**472**

Gimme five places on your body you would consider getting a tattoo

**473**

Gimme five items that operate with automatic timers

**474**

Gimme five cell phone features

**475**

Gimme five super powers you wish you had

**476**

Gimme five things that make you feel relaxed

**477**

Gimme five ways to get a baby to smile

**478**

Gimme five games you play with a glove

**479**

Gimme five things in almost every fairy tale

**480**

Gimme five things women (or men) like to do in groups

**481**

Gimme five things that frighten children at night

**482**

Gimme five of the worst places to receive a cell phone call

**483**

Gimme five things animals have that humans don't have

**484**

Gimme five things that are almost always red

**485**

Gimme five of the greatest inventions of all time

**486**

Gimme five places that have poorly maintained restrooms

**487**

Gimme five movies that make you cry

**488**

Gimme five foods that taste as good hot as cold

**489**

Gimme five movies that make you laugh

**490**

Gimme five foods people frequently eat in bed

**491**

Gimme five home appliances that make a lot of noise

## 492

Gimme five places where children get separated from their parents

## 493

Gimme five reasons to live to a really old age

**FOLLOW-UPS:**

How many years do you want to live?

How do you feel about the age you are right now?

If you had to be one age for the rest of your life, what age would you choose?

How old do you think you will live to be?

## 494

Gimme five situations that cause siblings to fight

**495**

Gimme five items kids take to the park


**496**

Gimme five objects parents should keep away
from their children


**497**

Gimme five cell phone ring tones


**498**

Gimme five movies with actors who play more
than one part


**499**

Gimme five uses for duct tape

# GIMME FIVE

## 500

Gimme five excuses teenagers give their parents for coming home late

## 501

Gimme five classes you wish your school would offer

## 502

Gimme five ways to ask your parents for money

## 503

Gimme five things you can sleep on besides a bed

**FOLLOW-UPS:**

What position do you sleep in? (e.g., on your back, on your side, etc.)

What's a comfortable temperature for sleeping? Why?

## 504

Gimme five of the best Halloween costumes

## 505

Gimme five of the worst Halloween costumes

## 506

Gimme five of the best comic book villains

## 507

Gimme five ingredients in cake

# GIMME FIVE

**508**

Gimme five qualities you look for in a friend

**509**

Gimme five things to do while baby-sitting

**510**

Gimme five of the lamest cars ever made

**511**

Gimme five band reunions you'd pay big money to witness

**512**

Gimme five colors in a crayon box

**513**

Gimme five one–hit–wonder bands from the '80s (or '90s or '00s, etc.)

**514**

Gimme five ocean activities

**515**

Gimme five advertising slogans that get stuck in your head

**516**

Gimme five songs you never want to hear on the radio again

**517**

Gimme five games to play in the rain

518

Gimme five military ranks

519

Gimme five reasons to end a friendship

520

Gimme five things that grow on vines

521

Gimme five things you eat off a stick

522

Gimme five places you can go at 3 a.m.

523

Gimme five things you need a helmet for

## 524

Gimme five inedible things kids often swallow

## 525

Gimme five occasions during which it'd be inappropriate to fall asleep

## 526

Gimme five verbal greetings

## 527

Gimme five famous cowboys

## 528

Gimme five things you could do to pass the time while stuck in an elevator

**529**

Gimme five beach activities

**530**

Gimme five things you run from

**531**

Gimme five names for God

**532**

Gimme five types of dip

**533**

Gimme five ways to ask someone out

**534**

Gimme five ways to ask someone to marry you

**535**

Gimme five things to put on your feet

**536**

Gimme five things to do with a straw

**537**

Gimme five things to do with balloons

**538**

Gimme five songs you sang in preschool

**539**

Gimme five jobs that require a uniform

**540**

Gimme five inappropriate words or phrases to say on an airplane

# GIMME FIVE

**541**

Gimme five nocturnal animals

**542**

Gimme five types of fabric

**543**

Gimme five childhood memories

**544**

Gimme five electronic appliances for listening to music

**545**

Gimme five ways to break up with your boyfriend/girlfriend

**546**

Gimme five sports you rarely see on TV

**547**

Gimme five things to do while you're bored in class

**548**

Gimme five things to do in the library

**549**

Gimme five things to do in a doctor's waiting room

**550**

Gimme five things to do when you're grounded

**551**

Gimme five attractions at Disney World

**552**

Gimme five things to do with dogs you're pet-sitting

**553**

Gimme five things to do for your mother (or father) when she's (or he's) sad

**554**

Gimme five things to do when you lose your voice

**555**

Gimme five things to do to an annoying younger sibling

**556**

Gimme five things you do while you're putting off homework

**557**

Gimme five things to do instead of watching TV

**558**

Gimme five words that have *ick* in them

**559**

Gimme five elements on the periodic table

**560**

Gimme five MTV hosts (past or present)

**561**

Gimme five NFL teams (or NBA or MLB or NHL)

**562**

Gimme five slang words that mean "to kiss"

**563**

Gimme five variations on the game of volleyball

**564**

Gimme five snow-related activities

**565**

Gimme five reasons to cancel a date

# WORD INDEX

(**NOTE:** Numbers refer to item entries within book—1 to 565—*not* to page numbers.)

# GIMME FIVE

# TOPICAL INDEX

(**NOTE:** Numbers refer to item entries within book—1 to 565—*not* to page numbers.)